<u>Easy Walks in</u>
<u>Massachusetts</u>

Bellingham, Blackstone, Franklin, Hopedale, Medway, Milford, Millis, Uxbridge, Wrentham, and Woonsocket, RI

Marjorie Turner Hollman

Easy Walks in Massachusetts: Bellingham, Blackstone, Franklin, Hopedale, Medway, Milford, Millis, Uxbridge, Wrentham, and Woonsocket, RI

1. Non-fiction 2. Outdoors 3. Hiking 4. Biking

5. Family activities 6. Southern New England outdoor activities

Silver Lake Publications

Bellingham, MA 02019

www.marjorieturner.com

Silver Lake Publications

Acknowledgments

Many walking partners helped make this book possible. They not only made the exploratory trips more fun, but they also provided the support I needed as I returned to trails to document details of each location. Hiking partners included (alphabetically) Sam Bettencourt, Amanda Coakley, Maud Dillingham, Beth Farwell, my husband Jon Hollman, Donna Johnson, Carolle Lawson, Catherine Mazuroski, Beth Nelson, Jennifer Powell, Anna, Nicole and David Rogers, and Cassandra Seyffert.

Pam Johnson of the Bellingham Bulletin granted permission for use of material from local hiking trail articles (titled "Naturally New England") I originally wrote for the Bulletin in 2010. The digital icons used in this book were open-sourced from clker.com. Editing by Em Turner Chitty, EmturnerEnglish.com.

Table of Contents

Introduction

New England is rich in history. Clues of past settlement are evident near many trails in this guide—stone foundations, cellar holes and stone walls.

Trails included are in the Upper Charles and Blackstone River watersheds, just north of the Massachusetts-Northern Rhode Island border. The Blackstone River Bikeway (also included here) is in northern Rhode Island. One of my favorite bike rides, I could not leave this gem out.

Unless indicated, the trails listed here are not handicapped accessible, strollers are usable only at railtrails and Hopedale Parklands. Several railtrails are open for walking, running, biking, and roller-blading. Some trails allow horseback riding.

A few canoe and kayak access points are mentioned, but walks are the primary focus of this book. GPS coordinates are approximate, derived from Google Earth. Distances noted are also approximate.

There are additional trails in some towns which are not included here. Some are not well-marked. Others are overrun by dirt bikes, or have become overgrown and difficult to follow. If you know of trails not included in this guide and you think they should be, please let me know!

Marjorie Turner Hollman

marjorie@marjorieturner.com

April, 2014

Words of Caution

Conditions of access, and trail conditions may change at any time. Rights of access (parking, trail routes) cannot be guaranteed. Never block roads, gates, or access points. "People" trails exist which stray off of known town or accessible properties. Please respect all posted and private property.

Use common sense while outdoors. Wear comfortable, closed-toe shoes that protect your feet. Bring water, preferably in a light backpack to leave your hands free. Hats are helpful. Windbreakers and/or raincoats can make the difference between a fun walk and a miserable time. Dress in layers.

While these hikes are all relatively easy, falls, trip hazards, sliding on wet rocks, and more are still possible. Keep your eyes open. Horseplay on rocks and trails can have tragic consequences.

Learn to recognize poison ivy, which is ubiquitous in the eastern U.S. The hairy roots of poison ivy climb many trees, are sometimes huge, and are just as noxious as the foliage. Winter is no protection, so use caution. Technu and Zanfel are helpful to fend off the worst effects of this plant.

If you are hiking alone, let someone know where you are going! Avoid taking walks close to dusk. The sun sets quickly in winter, and a dark, unfamiliar trail is a perfect opportunity for injury. Carry a flashlight in your pack just in case. Don't treat the outdoors as a place where "carefree" means "careless."

With these words of caution, please get outside and have fun!

KEY

wheelchair accessible

restroom at site, seasonal

site has designated parking

no designated parking

paved bicycle trail

unimproved mountain-
bike trail

horse trail

known motorbike problem

canoe access

swimming beach

no dogs allowed

dogs must be leashed

fishing permitted

Bellingham

BELLINGHAM

Arcand Park

Notable: Boat launch at edge of pond for non-motorized boats. Fishing. Swimming beach, no lifeguards.

Trail Map: None available presently.

GPS Coordinates: 42°2'0.56"N, 71°28'13.88"W

Directions: From intersection of Rtes. 140 and 126, (Bellingham Center), travel south on Rt. 126 for 1 mile. Turn left at Center St. (across from VFW Hall). Drive 2 miles to intersection of Center St and Pulaski Blvd. Turn left at light onto Pulaski, .25 miles to

BELLINGHAM

right at Lake St., turn right. Gated entrance to park is immediately on right.

Cost: Permit required for parking from Memorial Day to Labor Day. Permit is free to Bellingham residents, non-residents pay $40 for parking permit, obtained at Bellingham DPW (open weekdays) on Blackstone St. Permit good for both Silver Lake and Arcand Park.

Bathrooms: Not open.

Best time to visit: April-November. Park-beach area closed in winter (December-March).

Trail Conditions: Unimproved, clear, walkable dirt track, some varied terrain, muddy in places.

Distance: Trail network is about .75 mile.

Arcand Park is a town-owned recreation facility that is open seasonally. Unpaved trails are on the far side of the pond, opposite the parking area and swimming beach. Swim at own risk: no lifeguards.

Follow the shoreline around past the small dam till you find several spots where trails head off into the woods, away from the shore. Watch for poison ivy, especially along the shoreline. Network of trails leading into the woods is not good for biking, but fine for walking with children, exercising dogs and exploring in the woods. No dogs allowed in swimming area.

Spring to fall, gate opens at 8AM and closes at 7PM. Port-a-Potties available when open. A great place to practice paddling kayaks; wear flotation devices while boating.

BELLINGHAM

SNETT Bellingham

Notable: Portion of the SNETT (Southern New England Trunkline Trail). Features rock cuts, farm views. Proposed railrail, under development.

Trail Map: Available from Mass.gov website—Division of Conservation and Recreation (DCR).

GPS Coordinates: 42°2'46.28"N, 71°28'31.17"W (Center St.) 42°3'19.24"N, 71°27'43.07"W (Lake St.)

Directions: From Rt. 495, Exit 18 Bellingham Rt. 126, travel south on Rt. 126 2 miles to intersection of Rtes. 126 and 140 (Bellingham Center). Continue south on Rt. 126 1 mile. Turn left at Center St.

BELLINGHAM

(across from VFW Hall). Just over 1 mile down on Center St., look for SNETT parking signs on right, just before Fox Run Road.

Additional parking access on Lake St., just south of Cross St., between Pulaski Blvd. and S. Maple St.

Cost: None.

Bathrooms: None.

Best time to visit: Year round, opportunity for cross-country skiing in winter.

Trail Conditions: Wide, unimproved former railbed has sandy and soft spots, large dirt humps from dirt bike usage. Trail from Center St. west to Rt. 126 is mostly wet and inaccessible.

Distance: From Center St. to Franklin line about 1.5 miles in length.

From the Center St. kiosk, cross Center St. on the designated crosswalk and look for a rudimentary trail indicated from the street to the SNETT. A gate has been installed to discourage motorized vehicles, prohibited on all DCR trails.

Near the Sportsman's Club, the trail crosses Lake St. Use caution crossing at this point—sight lines are limited. Designated parking on Lake St. as well as crosswalks and pedestrian signs have heightened awareness, but speeding cars are a serious concern.

On the other side of Lake St. are farm fields and woodlands. Look for the "bossy crossing" (an underpass) built at the time the railroad was constructed so the Crooks family cows could access farmland on the other side of the tracks from where the main farm continues to operate.

BELLINGHAM

North Maple Street-Charles River

Notable: Small waterfall at trailhead. Access point to walk along Upper Charles River. Waterfowl can often be spotted in the river. Power plant property nearby is off-limits. Do not trespass! Beware hunters during hunting season.

Trail Map: None available presently.

GPS Coordinates: 42°2'9.11"N, 71°27'59.71"W

Directions: 495, exit 18, Rt. 126, head north toward Medway .5 mile past shopping centers. Next light is Maple St. (just before Stall Brook School). At .25 mile, turn right just before guardrail at small pull-off across from Scandia Kitchens. No signs to indicate parking.

Cost: None.

Bathrooms: None.

Best time to visit: Year round, but trails less accessible in spring because of flooding; area used by hunters during hunting season in the fall.

Trail Conditions: Wide, unimproved track, wet near trailhead in spring.

Distance: .33+ miles, network of trails, avoid power plant property due south of trailhead. Do not trespass!

The Charles River flows past an old mill building (presently housing Scandia Kitchens) as it crosses under N. Maple St., very close to Rt. 126 in North Bellingham. Across the street from the mill is land owned by the Army Corps of Engineers, on the north bank of the river, where there is space for 2-3 cars. Do not impede access to the dam. Conservation land is on the south side of the river.

Small seasonal streams present a barrier to the network of trails beyond the trailhead, but the water dries up in the fall. The paths beyond the dam bring you down next to the river.

The Charles River is still relatively small as it wends its way through Bellingham on its way to Boston. The Upper Charles begins in Hopkinton and several trails included in this book offer views of the sometimes elusive river. Years ago, these small waterways were potential sources of power. Remnants of an old dam are evident near the trailhead.

BELLINGHAM

High Street Ball Field

Notable: Secluded spot on the Charles River, very picturesque. Numerous side trails lead into marshland and Charles River floodplain. Opportunity for cross-country skiing.

Trail Map: None available presently.

GPS Coordinates: 42°5'37.91"N, 71°28'11.84"W

BELLINGHAM

Directions: From Rtes. 140 and 126 (Bellingham Center), take Rt. 126 (N. Main St.) north to blinking light, .25 mile, turn right onto High St., continue .5 mile to ball fields on right.

Cost: None.

Bathrooms: Next to ball fields, open during events.

Best time to visit: Year round. Insect repellent needed except in late fall and winter.

Trail conditions: Broad, relatively level unimproved track. Easy walking, but several forks in trail, some lead off into marshy areas. Head due south to reach river. No trail markings.

Distance: About .5 mile from trailhead to banks of the Charles River.

To access the trailhead, walk toward the ball field on the far right near the woods and look for the tall black bat boxes. A small sign notes that this is a walking trail, but it is not prominent. The trail leads toward a substantial floodplain of the Charles River as well as the banks of the river itself. Mosquito repellent is a necessity until frost.

A footbridge over an intermittent seasonal stream is slated for construction in 2014. The path has few rocks or tree roots. There are no trail markings, and off-road vehicles have created numerous side tracks that can be confusing.

The trails are unmarked. By avoiding the "people trails" that go to houses at the edge of the area (on right while walking away from the trailhead) and head due south, the trail goes to a spot on the banks of the Charles River. The river is quite shallow and about eight feet across. The river embankment is quite steep.

BELLINGHAM

Stall Brook School

Notable: Rock outcroppings and pond. The Stall Brook flows by the trailhead. An old Army bridge provides access over the brook.

Trail Map: None available presently.

GPS Coordinates: 42°7'21.00"N, 71°27'26.28"W

Directions: Rt. 495, exit 18, head north on Rt.126 for .5 mile past shopping centers. Next light is Maple St. Just past light is Stall Brook Elementary School on left. Parking is in back, to the far right of the school.

Cost: None.

BELLINGHAM

<u>Bathrooms</u>: None.

<u>Best time to visit</u>: After-school hours only, no access when school is open.

<u>Trail Conditions</u>: Unimproved dirt track, easy, wide, unpaved trails through pine woods, some tree roots and rocks in path.

<u>Distance</u>: Network of trails, about 1 mile.

Park in designated trail lot to the right of the school, around the back, next to the bridge that spans the Stall Brook. This old Army surplus bridge was installed in the 1970s when teachers at Stall Brook School wanted to create a walking trail for the students' use.

Parking and access are on school property. Public use of the trail is limited to when school is not in session and after 4 pm on school days.

After crossing the bridge, travel along the edge of the wetlands for a short distance near the brook. The path soon turns to the left and follows an old stone wall for much of the approximately mile long trail. The main path is wide and easy to follow, with some roots in the walkways.

Alternatively, while on the main path, look for a somewhat smaller trail to the right. This will lead you to a pond and additional trails.

BELLINGHAM

Silver Lake Park

Notable: Playground. Easy boat put-in at beach area for kayaks and canoes. Migrating waterfowl in fall and spring. Swimming, no lifeguards.

Trail Map: None available presently.

GPS Coordinates: 42°3'33.31"N, 71°27'54.65"W

Directions: From intersection of Rtes. 140 and 126 (Bellingham Center) head south on Rt. 126. Turn left at Center St. (across from VFW Hall); next left (.25

mile) is Cross St. Travel .5 mile on Cross St. to Silver Lake Park, on left.

<u>Cost</u>: Permit required for parking from Memorial Day to Labor Day. Permit free to Bellingham residents; non-residents pay $40 for parking permit, obtained at DPW on Blackstone St. Permit good for both Silver Lake and Arcand Park.

<u>Bathrooms</u>: Port-a-Potties.

<u>Best time to visit</u>: The park-beach area is closed in winter (December-March).

<u>Trail Conditions</u>: Paths on island are very overgrown, accessible only by boat. Walking in park itself is flat parkland.

<u>Distance</u>: 60 acre park, includes lake.

This quiet pond offers summer swimming (no lifeguards, swim at own risk) and novice experiences with canoes or kayaks. No motorized boats over 10HP are allowed. If you have a boat you may want to head to the island in the middle of the lake, where there are paths that travel the length of the island.

Late July and early August are great times for blueberrying. Because the island has become overgrown, most fruit is hanging over the water; berry picking from a canoe or kayak is your best bet to get enough blueberries for a pancake supper.

There is a playground at Silver Lake that offers opportunities for energetic children to climb, swing, slide, and more.

Watch for great blue herons, kingfishers, swans, mallards, occasional osprey, and migrating waterfowl in the spring and fall.

BELLINGHAM

Bellingham Town Common

Notable: Playground and circular walking paths, historical markers.

Trail Map: None available presently.

GPS Coordinates: 42°5'16.19"N, 71°28'37.41"W

Directions: Rt. 495, exit 18 Bellingham 126. Travel south on Rt. 126 2 miles to intersection of Rtes. 126 and 140 (Bellingham Center). The common will be on your right just before intersection of Rtes. 140 and 126.

Cost: None.

BELLINGHAM

Bathrooms: Port-a-Potties in far corner next to gas station.

Best time to visit: Open year round, dawn to dusk.

Trail Conditions: Paved walkways, handicapped accessible.

Distance: Several acre park.

The Bellingham Town Common is a modern creation, constructed in 1997 on a site that was once an old dairy farm and more recently a grocery store. At the intersection of Rtes. 140 and 126, the Bellingham Common is truly in the center of Bellingham.

There is a network of paved walking paths as well as a small playground tucked into the back corner away from traffic. There is adequate parking during most times of day unless a town-wide event is underway. Parking is just before the intersection of 126 and 140 on North Main St., or on Rte 140 (Mendon St.) just before reaching the center of town coming from the Mendon/Milford direction.

Look for granite historical markers along all the walkways, with photos of Bellingham in days gone by. Many of the photos are of the area immediately surrounding the common and reflect changes in the community.

Benches offer comfortable places for parents to rest while children enjoy the playground. Dogs and skateboards are prohibited. There are Port-a-Potties along the far edge of the common, in the direction of the gas station on North Main St. (Rt. 126) just before you reach the common.

Blackstone

BLACKSTONE

Blackstone Gorge

Notable: Most difficult trail listed in this book. Views of the river, boat ramp for river access just above the dam. Part of the Blackstone River Valley Heritage Corridor.

Trail Map: Blackstone River Valley Heritage Corridor trail maps available from Mass.gov website—Division of Conservation and Recreation (DCR)

GPS Coordinates: 42°0'55.25"N, 71°33'9.33"W

Directions: Intersection of Rtes. 16 and 122 (Uxbridge Center), take Rt. 122 south 2 miles down, look for brown "Blackstone Gorge" sign on the right

BLACKSTONE

at County St. and turn right. At end of County St., large parking lot is on left; the Blackstone River (which created the gorge) is directly at end of street.

Cost: None.

Bathrooms: None.

Best time to visit: Year round.

Trail Conditions: Rigorous, rocky, hilly hiking trail with some steep exposures to river.

Distance: From trailhead to peak of trail, about .5 mile. More trails beyond the highest rocks along the river, but may traverse private property.

The rocky, unmarked, well-worn paths beside the river are challenging to walk, filled with boulders, roots, and sections that require clambering over rocky spots that may be slippery. The walkway slowly climbs upward, ultimately reaching 80 feet above the river. The steep cliffs of the Gorge offer scenes of spectacular beauty in every season.

Just above the dam is a quiet section of river, accessed by a boat ramp next to the dam. The gate to the boat ramp is blocked off. Expect to haul canoe or kayak about twenty yards to the water's edge.

To the north upstream is the triad bridge, future crossing for the SNETT in Millville. The river is populated by numerous herons, kingfishers, osprey and other waterfowl. Beware strong spring currents.

The barrels in front of the dam are sometimes dislodged by floodwaters; use care when returning to the shore—the boat ramp is quite near the edge of the dam. A power plant water intake is just upstream. The intake current becomes quite strong close to the plant—heed warning signs when boating!

<u>Franklin</u>

FRANKLIN

Beaver Pond (Chilson Beach)

Notable: Look for signs of beaver and migrating waterfowl.

Trail Map: Not available presently.

GPS Coordinates: 42°4'57.39"N, 71°25'5.38"W

Directions: Rt. 495 exit 17, Franklin Rt. 140, travel toward Franklin Center on Rt. 140 for .75 mile. At stop light, turn right on Beaver St. just past Akin Back Farm. Beaver Pond is .5 mile down on left, just before the 495 overpass.

Cost: Chilson Beach pass for Memorial Day to Labor Day, for Franklin residents only, $75.

FRANKLIN

<u>Bathrooms</u>: Summer only.

<u>Best time to visit</u>: For Franklin residents only during the summer; swimming and boating. Year-round for hiking, no residential restrictions before Memorial Day and after Labor Day.

<u>Trail conditions</u>: Unimproved, wide dirt track.

<u>Distance</u>: .25 mile.

The sounds of Rt. 495 are inescapable, but Beaver Pond still offers a nice, easy walk and plenty of parking. Also called Chilson Beach, the pond area posts lifeguards in the summer, offers swimming and ball fields, but beyond the beach area on the left (the east side of the pond, away from Rt. 495) there is a trail that follows the edge of the pond.

The trail intersects Beaver Pond and a marsh area, which lies on the other side of the trail. Lots of opportunity for birding. The trail dead-ends in a water department access road. There is no public access in or out of this road.

About three-fourths of the way to the end of the trail, another trail branches off to the left along the edges of the marsh—follow it around the marsh edge to see multiple signs of beaver, appropriate for a recreation area on Beaver St.! Parts of the trail are somewhat obstructed by beaver activity, but still fun to explore with children, who may discover the tell-tale signs of beaver's presence.

FRANKLIN

Dacey Athletic Fields

Notable: Brook with board walks; 18-hole disc golf course. Circular trail.

Trail Map: Not available presently.

GPS Coordinates: 42°7'12.81"N, 71°23'56.89"W

Directions: At Franklin's town common, Main St. is to the right of St. Mary's Church. Take Main Street away from the downtown .2 mile, bear right at the little red schoolhouse to stay on Lincoln St. for about 2 miles, go past elementary and middle school on left, and Dacey Athletic Fields are on the next left, .5 mile past school complex. Trailhead is just to the left

FRANKLIN

of the fenced-in dog park area. Look for sign for Dacey Disc Golf Course.

Cost: None.

Bathrooms: Port-a-Potties at field near parking lot.

Best time to visit: Accessible year round.

Trail conditions: Narrow boardwalks, wide, unimproved trails, roots and rocks in trail, relatively flat.

Distance: A network of trails makes distance variable. Less than a mile.

The woodland trails behind the sports fields have been developed as a "disc golf course." (little plastic discs tossed at targets). This network of trails now has arrows indicating where the "golf course" trail goes, but the trail is still essentially a large loop that crosses a small stream several times as it flows through the area. A series of boardwalks enable walkers to get through muddy areas of the trail.

A dog park has recently been added to the Dacey Athletic Fields complex. Dogs are permitted at the dog park and on leashes on the trails. No dogs on athletic fields.

The Recreation Department has posted multiple warnings on its website against sledding at the Dacey field complex. Insect repellent is advisable in warmer weather.

FRANKLIN

Indian Rock Conservation Area

Notable: Large rock outcropping. Trails not maintained.

Trail Map: Not available presently.

GPS Coordinates: 42°5'15.67"N, 71°22'10.31"W

Directions: From downtown Franklin center, take Rt. 140 (E. Central St.) head east .5 mile, turn left at light, Chestnut St., go .75 mile to Jordan Road on right. .25 mile along Jordan Road, turn left onto Indian Lane. Take first left onto King Philip Road, a dead end, park at end of road, look left for small conservation marker on tree, opening onto the trail.

Cost: None.

Bathrooms: None.

Best time to visit: Year round; insect repellent in summer.

Trail Conditions: Unimproved, dirt track, fallen trees impede trails.

Distance: .25 mile to Indian Rock, additional small network of trails, not maintained or marked.

Access to this property is at the end of a residential dead-end street. There is no designated parking. Avoid blocking neighbor's driveways.

Indian Rock is a small parcel of conservation land that is worth visiting for the fun of clambering on the large rock outcropping that is quite near the trailhead. There is no sign marking the trailhead at present, but there is a small round "Franklin Conservation Commission" marker on a tree quite near the street where the trail opens up.

Only a few yards after entering the woods at the trailhead, look for the trail toward Indian Rock on the right. Follow the well-worn path to the rock outcrop, but beware—when standing on top of the rock there is a substantial drop to the ground below at the edge of the outcrop.

The oak-hemlock forest has grown up and blocks the view except in winter. There is a smaller, obstructed path to the base of the rock.

FRANKLIN

Delcarte Conservation Area

Notable: Water views, several ponds.

Trail Map: At kiosk at trailhead.

GPS Coordinates: 42°5'39.85"N, 71°23'10.02"W (Flintlocke entrance) 42°5'54.56"N, 71°22'50.81"W (Greystone entrance)

FRANKLIN

<u>Directions</u>: From Franklin's town common, take Pleasant St. toward Norfolk about 1 mile. Two entrances: First entrance, on right opposite Flintlocke Road; second entrance, .5 mile on right, opposite Greystone Road. Del Carte Conservation Area signs at parking lots. Parking kiosk has trail map.

<u>Cost</u>: None.

<u>Bathrooms</u>: None.

<u>Best time to visit</u>: Year round.

<u>Trail Conditions</u>: Narrow, unimproved dirt track, boardwalks through muddy areas.

<u>Distance</u>: .5 mile trail, more being developed.

Parking is directly on Pleasant St. in two good parking lots with clear signage. The parking and trailhead across from Greystone St. has a playground and picnic tables.

This 136-acre property is managed by the Franklin Conservation Commission. Several dams, recently restored, form the ponds on the property.

A few rolling sections of the trail are easily traversable. Wood chips and a small bridge over a tiny stream make for dry paths with solid footing. Small boat ramp for canoes and kayaks at parking area across from Greystone St. Fishing is catch and release only.

FRANKLIN

SNETT Franklin

Notable: This section of the SNETT (Southern New England Trunkline Trail) railtrail is mostly graded and cleared, and still being developed. Stone retaining walls, steep slopes to woods below the trail.

Trail Map: Available from Mass.gov website—Division of Conservation and Recreation (DCR).

GPS Coordinates: 42°3'43.06"N, 71°25'42.55"W

Directions: Rt. 495 exit 17, Rt. 140, Franklin, head toward Bellingham, Grove St is immediately past interchange, turn left at light. Follow Grove St. 2 miles, look for SNETT signs, parking on left, trailhead on right.

Cost: None.

FRANKLIN

Bathrooms: None.

Best time to visit: Year round. Cross-country skiing in winter.

Trail conditions: Wide, flat, unimproved former railbed. Steep climb up and over Prospect St. where trail is obstructed. Moguls created by dirt bikes. Graded from Grove St. to Spring St.

Distance: About 1.5 miles from Grove St. to Bellingham line.

This mostly unimproved former rail bed/right of way is owned by the Mass. Dept of Conservation and Recreation (DCR), extending from Franklin through Bellingham, Blackstone, Millville, Uxbridge, and into Douglas. Poor drainage due to removal of the original rail ballast, and "humps" caused by prohibited off-track vehicles poses both minor and major challenges in various sections.

The easternmost section in Franklin is graded (2013) but is otherwise unimproved. Proceeding west, the trail crosses Spring St and open farmland in just over half a mile. Watch for poison ivy. At about the 1-mile mark the trail is blocked by a 20-foot high infill where Prospect St crosses the trail. Stay off residential property and driveways.

From Prospect St. there is a .5 mile unimproved but passable stretch to the Lake St. Bellingham parking area. This section of the path offers 20-foot high rock cuts with original drill marks. The boundary between the Bellingham and Franklin sections of the trail is unmarked.

<u>Hopedale</u>

HOPEDALE

Hopedale Parklands

Notable: Stone bridge, boat put-in at main entrance (Dutcher/Hopedale St.) in spring only during high water. Carriage paths encircle most of pond, water views. Large glacial boulders. Swimming in summer, lifeguards posted.

Trail Map: Available through internet search.

GPS Coordinates: 42° 8'6.94"N, 71°32'38.71"W (main entrance) 42°8'8.22"N, 71°33'8.33"W (Freedom St. entrance) 42°8'53.40"N, 71°33'26.50"W (Hazel St.)

Directions: Three entrances: 162 Dutcher St. (intersection with Hopedale St.), Hazel St., Freedom St. Details at end of section.

HOPEDALE

Cost: None.

Bathrooms: Available summer only, beach area on Dutcher/Hopedale St.

Best time to visit: Year-round. Opportunity for cross-country skiing. Water in pond low in summer and fall.

Trail Conditions: Wide, well-marked, graded, unpaved carriage path, some rocks, tree roots.

Distance: About 2.25 miles to circle pond, but must travel on street to complete a loop.

Hopedale Parklands, or "The Parklands," as it's locally known, is at 162 Dutcher St. in Hopedale, and offers over 2 miles of walking trails on 273 acres, which surround Hopedale Pond. The broad open pathways give one the sense of walking on the carriage trails of Acadia National Park. Baby carriages can navigate this trail.

The main entrance, where the town swimming beach is located, is at the intersection of Dutcher and Hopedale St., accessed directly from Route 16.

Each entrance has a different feel to it. The main entrance is more heavily used. The Hazel St. entrance is the most remote, requiring a quarter-mile walk through woodland to reach the pond. The Freedom St. entrance is less-used than the entrance at Dutcher/Hopedale St., and has some ups and downs, but follows the shoreline closely.

Broad trails offer lots of room to run. Picnic tables and benches on the Dutcher/Hopedale St. side of the Parklands. The Mill River flows under a stone bridge and feeds into the pond. The bridge is at about the half-way mark from either the Freedom St. or Dutcher/Hopedale St. entrances.

HOPEDALE

The wide walkway circumnavigating the pond is mostly a gravel path. Private property along the shore of the pond near the mill prevents a complete circumnavigation of the pond by footpath.

Dutcher/Hopedale St. entrance: From Rt. 140 northbound, in Milford, turn left onto Rt. 16 westbound at the Milford Regional Medical Center, continue to the next light, turn right onto Hopedale St. Drive past Draper Mill complex to Freedom St. You will see the pond ahead on your left. Street parking is straight ahead, both sides of Hopedale St. up to Dutcher St. the actual address for the park.

Freedom St. entrance: Follow directions above to intersection of Hopedale and Freedom St. Turn left onto Freedom St., drive past Draper Mill about .1 mile. Freedom St. bears sharply right almost immediately past the mill. Just past a small neighborhood, about .2 mile is a gated entrance to the Parklands on the right with space for four cars.

Hazel St. entrance: Hazel St. is a short, dead-end road accessed from Route 140. From intersection of Rtes. 140 and 16 at Milford Hospital, continue toward Upton on Rt. 140 almost 2 miles. Hazel St. is on the left just before the Milford Geriatric Center. Near the end of Hazel St. is a yellow park gate and parking for about 7 cars. About .25 mile walk to pond from parking on Hazel St.

<u>Medway</u>

MEDWAY

Choate Park

Notable: Waterfall at entrance to park. Stone walls along woodland path from pond to Medway High School. Circular trail around pond.

Trail map: Not available presently.

GPS Coordinates: 42°8'52.98"N, 71°25'38.69"W

Directions: From intersection of Main St. and Highland Street, Rt. 109 in Medway (Medway Community Church), head northeast on Rt. 109 toward business district. At .2 mile, turn left onto Mechanic St., then quickly turn right at Oak St.

MEDWAY

Follow road past the Thayer House; parking is adjacent to park area.

Cost: None.

Bathrooms: Port-a-Potties next to ball fields adjacent to park.

Best time to visit: Year round. Parking lot is plowed in winter.

Trail Conditions: Wide, dirt track, graded around pond, unimproved between pond and high school.

Distance: Path around the pond is a little over .25 mile; path between the park and Medway High School is a little over .5 mile.

A fifteen-foot waterfall (part of Chicken Brook) cascades over the dam that created Choate Pond, right next to the parking area. Pond is open for swimming in summer, no lifeguards. High bacteria counts can close pond for swimming.

The walking path encircling the pond is a rolling, graded track. The trailhead, on the far side of Choate Pond, has a "Medway Open Space" blue sign, is level, with few tree roots, and leads directly to Medway High School.

MEDWAY

Charles River, Sanford Mills

Notable: Boat launch area at the Charles River, large flat rock in river, favorite sunning place for swimmers in years gone by. Circular trail.

Trail map: Not available presently.

GPS Coordinates: 42°8'23.22"N, 71°24'2.12"W

Directions: Village St. in Medway to Medway Town Hall, Sanford St. is adjacent to the town hall. Turn right onto Sanford St. Sanford Mills Condo Complex is on right, just behind the town hall. Turn into the driveway, stay to right, follow all the way to back of

MEDWAY

buildings, parking is on the far right, look for trailhead sign off the pavement, toward the river.

Cost: None.

Best time to visit: Year-round.

Trail conditions: Wide, unimproved dirt track, well-marked.

Distance: About 50 yards to the river, trail follows a loop in area formerly known as the "Amphitheater." Loop about .25 mile in length.

The only access to this trail along the Charles River is through a private condominium complex, the Sanford Mill. Park only in designated trail parking spots and make sure other cars are not blocked. Although access is by way of private property, the town has legal easement to the conservation property with frontage on the Charles River.

This trail is part of what was once the town picnic area called "The Amphitheater," directly behind the Medway Town Hall on Village St. Thanks to the efforts of local volunteers and Medway Conservation Commission members, invasive plants that once choked the four-acre parcel have been removed. There are now trails and a small boat ramp available. The "Medway Open Space" sign directs you to the circular trail that takes you down to the river, along the shore a short distance, and then circles back to the beginning of the trailhead.

MEDWAY

Charles River, Village Street

Notable: Picnic tables, nice spot to lunch and explore along banks of the Charles River.

Trail map: Not available presently.

GPS Coordinates: 42°8'24.68"N, 71°25'31.30"W

Directions: Park at Medway Police Station, 315 Village St.

MEDWAY

Cost: None.

Best time to visit: Year-round.

Trail Conditions: Wide, graveled path.

Distance: 50 yards.

A quick walk brings you to a view of the Charles River on this very short trail. Medway Cub Scouts broadened the path and spread crushed stone on it. Several stone benches sit at the river's edge.

Parking is at the Police Station, 315 Village St. Park only in designated parking spots. Facing the station, look to the left for the opening to the trail, which is to the left of the parking lot, close to the street. The trail threads its way between the Police Station parking and the adjacent house, only a short walk to the Charles River. But it is indeed a trail, and the public is welcome to enjoy it.

MEDWAY

Idylwild Farm

Notable: Vernal pools in woods, stone walls, views of Chicken Brook.

Trail map: Not available presently.

GPS Coordinates: 42°10'10.09"N, 71°26'4.25"W

Directions: Rt. 109 Main St. in Medway to Winthrop St. Head north on Winthrop St. 1.5 miles to

MEDWAY

Partridge St. on left. Turn left onto Partridge St., continue straight onto Ward's Lane, and follow signs to Idylwild Fields about .3 mile. Two trailheads, one on the left as you park, the other to the far right of the athletic fields.

Cost: None.

Bathrooms: Port-a-Potties at edge of fields.

Best time to visit: Year round.

Trail Conditions: Wide, unimproved dirt track, some muddy spots.

Distance: Network of trails, .5 mile.

Idlywild Farms has a large athletic field with substantial parking available. There are two trailheads; to the far right is a network of trails with vernal pools and small seasonal streams that flow through the area. Trails are open and easily navigable.

The trail on the left leads directly to a beaver pond, part of Chicken Brook (which flows on into Choate Pond). The brook has a beaver dam that has created a good-sized pond. The trail loops around to the right and connects with the trail that starts on the opposite side of the athletic fields.

Milford

MILFORD

Upper Charles Trail

Notable: Louisa Lake, paved bicycle-walking railtrail, very popular.

Directions: Several parking areas: Fino Field in downtown Milford off Rt. 16, Main St. Louisa Lake on Dilla St.: 495 to exit 20, Rt. 85. Head toward Milford; first right is Dilla St. (presently a Wendy's restaurant at corner). Follow Dilla St. about 1 mile, look for bike crossing signs, parking is on right. From 495, Rt. 85 exit, travel 1.5 miles toward Hopkinton, parking is on right.

Trail Map: Available at Friends of the Milford Upper Charles Trail website.

GPS Coordinates: 42°9'22.28"N, 71°31'12.66"W (Louisa Lake) 42°11'17.64"N, 71°30'17.41"W (near Hopkinton line) 42°8'39.05"N, 71°30'48.58"W (Fino Field)

Cost: None

Bathrooms: None.

Best time to visit: Year round, but not plowed in winter. Opportunity for Cross Country skiing.

Trail conditions: Wide railtrail, paved bike path, mostly flat, pedestrian-marked road crossings.

Distance: About 3 miles.

The Upper Charles Trail originates in downtown Milford. Close to 3 miles at present, the paved trail is part of a planned non-motorized system that will eventually stretch from Milford to Framingham.

The trail through Milford offers water views of the Upper Charles River watershed. From Louisa Lake towards 495 there are lots of large boulders, and views of the Charles, which feeds into the lake. Near the downtown area the landscape is marshy, which attracts waterfowl. Signs warn of waterfowl hunting, so use caution during late fall months. There are benches along the trail.

The bike path crosses several streets, including an exit at Rt. 495. Care is needed; these are busy roads.

MILFORD

There are lots of walkers on this trail. If on bikes, give people verbal or bike-bell warning when you are approaching them.

If walking, observe signs that indicate which side of the trail you should stay on. Watch children to keep them to one side—many bikers use this trail.

There are now "QR" codes posted at the kiosks at trail entrances that can be used with smartphones. These codes provide trail maps and access to the Friends of Milford Upper Charles Trail Facebook page, which provides the most up-to-date information.

MILFORD

Upper Charles Trail Milford-Holliston

Notable: Milford section is paved railtrail. Stone bridges, marsh views. Holliston section is unpaved, graded but not compacted surface. Extremely limited parking at grade crossings in Holliston section.

Trail Map: Available at Friends of the Milford Upper Charles Trail website (only shows Milford section).

MILFORD

<u>Directions</u>: 495 to exit 19, Rt. 109, head west on Rt. 109 toward Milford, look for Friendly's restaurant .75 mile on left shortly before reaching Rt. 16. Trail parking is at the back of the Friendly's parking lot.

<u>GPS Coordinates</u>: 42° 8'56.46"N, 71°30'0.16"W

<u>Cost</u>: None.

<u>Bathrooms</u>: At Friendly's for customers.

<u>Best time to visit</u>: Year-round, unplowed in winter. Opportunity for cross-country skiing.

<u>Trail conditions</u>: Wide, paved railtrail bike path from Rt. 109 for first 1.5 miles. Remainer is mostly dirt, some stone dust, easy walking, some challenging biking because of loose gravel.

<u>Distance</u>: The paved portion of this trail starts at Rt. 109, continues under Rt. 495 and extends towards Holliston, about 1.5 miles. The Holliston section of this trail reaches to Holliston Center, about 5 miles, unpaved.

At press time, the beginning of this small, partially paved railtrail originates at the Friendly's parking lot. Look for parking spaces in the Friendly's lot that are designated for bike parking. An additional portion of the trail has been paved beyond the 495 underpass at Fortune Boulevard in Milford.

The path parallels Rt. 16 and continues to Holliston Center, intersecting Summer St. (Rt. 126) and smaller side streets. From the Holliston line up to Holliston Center the trail is a mostly graded stone dust path. Off the trail are large boulders, Army Corps of Engineers dam structures, numerous wetlands, and signs of beaver.

There are now "QR" codes posted at the kiosks at trail entrances that can be used with smartphones.

MILFORD

These codes provide trail maps and access to the Friend of Milford Bike Trail Facebook page, which provides more up-to-date information.

Construction is now underway on the one-mile link between the section that begins at the Hopkinton Town Line, and the portion of the trail that presently starts at Friendly's and ends just outside Holliston Center. The Milford section is overseen by the Friends of the Milford Upper Charles Trail. The Holliston section is overseen by the Friends of Holliston Trails.

Millis

MILLIS

Pleasant Meadow, formerly Verderber Farm

<u>Notable</u>: Views of back of Tangerini's Farm. Well marked, circular trails. Property managed to attract bluebirds in summer.

<u>Trail map</u>: Not available presently.

MILLIS

<u>Directions</u>: Address: 72 Pleasant St., Millis. From intersection of Rtes. 115 and 109 in Millis center, head west on Rt. 109 toward Medway .5 mile, turn left at light onto Pleasant St., .5 mile down, look on left for small sign for conservation property.

<u>GPS Coordinates</u>: 42°9'38.68"N, 71°21'55.46"W

<u>Cost</u>: None.

<u>Best time to visit</u>: Year round, but may be difficult to access in the winter.

<u>Trail Conditions</u>: Wide, unimproved track, well marked paths, rolling terrain.

<u>Distance</u>: About .5 mile loop, several additional trails through wooded area.

This 37 plus acre property abuts Tangerini Farm in Millis, which provides a substantial corridor for wildlife. About .5 mile in length, the path offers several loops to follow which are all marked out with red, yellow or blue trail markers on trees, thanks to local Girl Scouts' efforts.

Enter through what appears to be a residential driveway to the graveled parking area. Once parked, look toward the wooded area for the "Trailhead" sign to begin your walk. There are a few trees that have fallen across the paths, but nothing that is too difficult to step over. The open fields on either side of the wooded area are mowed by the Millis Conservation Commission to maintain habitat needed by bluebirds and other bird species. Dog walkers must clean up after their dogs.

<u>Uxbridge</u>

UXBRIDGE

River Bend Farm

Notable: Gravel walking path, original towpath for historic Blackstone River Canal; stone bridges at Hartford Avenue, remnants of locks along canal route. Trail head is west of Blackstone River.

Trail Map: Blackstone River Valley Heritage Corridor trail maps available from Mass.gov website—Division of Conservation and Recreation (DCR).

Directions: Address: 287 Oak St. Uxbridge. From Rt. 16, Uxbridge center travel east .2 mile to Oak St. Turn left; at .3 mile on Oak St., road forks near high school. Take right fork to stay on Oak, then drive .75 mile, large red barn, visitor's center on right.

UXBRIDGE

GPS Coordinates: 42° 5'38.82"N, 71°37'25.46"W

Cost: None. Special programs may have cost.

Bathrooms: At Visitor's Center, 10AM-4PM daily.

Best time to visit: Year round.

Trail Conditions: Unimproved flat towpath. Additional trails are unimproved dirt tracks.

Distance: Canal towpath next to farm from Hartford Avenue to Rt. 16 Stanley Woolen Mills, 1 mile.

All Uxbridge trails included in this publication except for the SNETT and West Hill Dam link to each other and are easily accessed on foot from any single parking location for the more enterprising walker.

Easy canoe and kayak access to the canal beside the Visitor's Center. Additional, less-traveled paths follow the banks of the Blackstone River itself.

Cross the bridge to the towpath, and either turn left or right to walk the towpath itself, or go almost straight across the towpath bridge onto trails along a large field opposite the Visitor's Center and head toward the river, on your left as you face the field.

Towpath is unpaved, free of rocks and roots. No fences or railings between the path and canal, which in places has a steep embankment. There are two arched, stone bridges at Hartford Avenue, under which the Blackstone River flows. The Blackstone River tends to run quite high in the spring, but generally is much quieter the rest of the year. Benches along the towpath offer rest to weary walkers.

UXBRIDGE

Lookout Rock

Notable: Views of the Blackstone River Valley. Trailhead is east of Blackstone River.

Trail Map: Blackstone River Valley Heritage Corridor trail maps available from Mass.gov website—Division of Conservation and Recreation (DCR).

GPS Coordinates: 42°6'51.33"N, 71°37'6.94"W

UXBRIDGE

<u>Directions</u>: From Mendon Center, intersection of Rt. 16 and North St., head west on Rt. 16; at .75 mile, turn right at Hartford Avenue (across from large auto dealerships in Mendon). Travel 2 miles to West Hill Dam entrance in Uxbridge. Continue past West Hill Dam another .5 mile, turn right onto Upton St., travel 1 mile to the T at Quaker St. Turn left at Quaker St., look for parking lot on left, .1 mile.

<u>GPS Coordinates</u>: 42°6'51.27"N, 71°37'6.37"W

<u>Cost</u>: None.

<u>Best time to visit</u>: Year round, beware hunters in fall.

<u>Trail conditions</u>: Unimproved dirt track, mostly level except for scramble up onto Lookout Rock itself.

<u>Distance</u>: .25 mile from parking to Lookout Rock.

Lookout Rock offers an unobstructed view of the Blackstone Valley, looking west from the vantage point of a rock outcropping.

There are a few signs of civilization when you get to the top of Lookout Rock, but this area offers a nice walk on easy paths to a broad view. The trails are pretty well marked, and only a little challenging in the fall when leaves cover the path. Upon arriving at the rock outcropping, use caution since there is a substantial drop from the top of the rock to the ground below.

Trails below the rock lead back along the Blackstone River to Rice City Pond.

UXBRIDGE

Rice City Pond

Notable: Views from east side of Blackstone River, wildlife. Trailhead is east of Blackstone River.

Trail Map: Blackstone Valley Heritage Corridor trail maps available from Mass.gov website—Division of Conservation and Recreation (DCR)

GPS Coordinates: 42°5'58.60"N, 71°37'9.59"W

Directions: From Mendon Center, intersection of Rt. 16 and North St., head west on Rt. 16. At .75 mile turn right at Hartford Avenue (across from large auto dealerships in Mendon), travel 2 miles to West Hill Dam entrance in Uxbridge. Pass West Hill Dam, another .5 mile, just before the Blackstone River, look on right for signs for Rice City Pond parking.

UXBRIDGE

<u>Cost</u>: None.

<u>Best time to visit</u>: Year round.

<u>Trail conditions</u>: Unimproved dirt track, mostly level, narrow in places along river.

<u>Distance</u>: 1 mile from parking at Hartford Avenue to Lookout Rock, just off Quaker St.

Just beyond West Hill Dam on Hartford Avenue in Uxbridge is a large parking area and sign for Rice City Pond. A stone bridge crosses the Blackstone River just beyond the parking area, with additional trails on the other side of the river. The east side of the river offers parking, picnic tables, access to the river, and a trail following the banks of the Blackstone.

The foot trail from Rice City pond eventually leads all the way to Lookout Rock if you continue to follow the riverbank for about 1 mile.

While walking this trail, you may see turtles sunning themselves in shallow water and on fallen logs in the slow-flowing river. Look for signs of muskrats.

UXBRIDGE

Goat Hill

Notable: Blackstone canal lock remnants. Interesting boulders along trail, views of remnants of Blackstone River Canal tow path. Additional, more challenging trails up Goat Hill noted at kiosk at trail head. Trailhead is west of Blackstone River.

Trail Map: Kiosk with map at trailhead. Blackstone Valley Heritage Corridor trail maps available from Mass.gov website—Division of Conservation and Recreation (DCR)

GPS Coordinates: 42°5'53.74"N, 71°37'27.64"W

Directions: From Mendon Center, intersection of Rt. 16 and North St., head west on Rt. 16. At .75 mile,

UXBRIDGE

turn right at Hartford Avenue (across from large auto dealerships in Mendon) and travel 2 miles to West Hill Dam entrance in Uxbridge. Pass West Hill Dam, another .5 mile, go pass signs for Rice City Pond parking, cross narrow bridge. Just past the bridge, look on right for trailhead. Alternate parking at Tri-River Health Center, 280 Hartford Avenue, Uxbridge, across the street from trailhead.

Cost: None.

Best time to visit: Year round.

Trail Conditions: Unimproved dirt track, mostly level.

Distance: .3 mile, to canal lock.

It is possible to track remnants of the Blackstone Canal towpath as you walk on this trail, but the towpath itself is overgrown, and the river has washed away most access. It appears in Rice City Pond as a curious straight, long stretch of land, just a few feet off shore from the trail.

Be mindful of the house that sits directly at Hartford Avenue next to Goat Hill trailhead. Parking is permitted in the field, but do not block the house driveway. You can also park safely at the Tri-River Health Clinic, directly across Hartford Avenue from the trailhead.

This trail offers a rare view of a canal lock, used to raise or lower water levels along the canal when it was in operation in the 1820s to 1840s. Locks are about ten feet wide, a somewhat surprising reminder of how narrow the barges that navigated through these passageways in the 1820's-1840's were. The barges carried cargo from Worcester to Pawtucket through the Blackstone Canal.

UXBRIDGE

About .3 mile from Hartford Avenue along the path, look for signs on the right that point to the lock. It's a steep scramble down off the main path, but worth the effort. There is a wooden bridge to access the towpath at this location. Granite blocks remain indicating the channel the boats had to traverse. After crossing the bridge, look at each end of the lock carefully. Wooden sluice gates were installed at each end and were raised or lowered to alter the water level, allowing boats to safely travel up or down the river despite changes in elevation.

The trail is named for the hill that rises steeply away from the banks of Rice City Pond. This is a popular area; so trails tend to be icy in the winter because of lots of foot traffic.

The trail along the river is open for quite some distance, but eventually becomes impassable. Trees prevent a clear view of the water from this trail. For better views, Lookout Rock can be reached from the other side of the river.

UXBRIDGE

West Hill Dam

Notable: Varied landscape, large dam, open, sunny areas, swimming area, wildlife. Trailhead is east of the Blackstone River. Circular trails.

Trail Map: At kiosk at swimming area, map also available on U.S. Army Corps of Engineers New England District website.

UXBRIDGE

GPS Coordinates: 42°6'8.01"N, 71°36'28.14"W (dam area) 42°6'45.95"N, 71°36'15.66"W (swimming area).

Directions: Address: 518 East Hartford Avenue, Uxbridge. From Mendon Center, intersection of Rt. 16 and North St., head west on Rt. 16. At .75 mile, turn right at Hartford Avenue (across from large auto dealerships in Mendon) and travel 2 miles to West Hill Dam entrance in Uxbridge on right.

Cost: Free if you park at the dam, fee in summer for swimming area off Quaker St.

Bathrooms: At ranger station, also Port-a-Potties near dam area. Seasonally, at swimming area.

Best time to visit: Dam area open year round; parking lot plowed in winter, swimming area open summer only.

Trail Conditions: Unimproved dirt track, roots and rocks on trail between dam and swimming area. Some open fields.

Distance: From dam to swimming area is .5 mile. Additional trails beyond swimming area.

West Hill Dam in Uxbridge is maintained by the U.S. Army Corps of Engineers and the parking lot at E. Hartford Ave. is maintained year round. This area, set aside for flood control, has become a nature preserve filled with trails.

Walk on the dam itself, next to the West River, or through woodlands, open fields and along marshy ponds. After parking at the Hartford Avenue entrance, continue straight into the woods and follow trails, or stop and investigate the dam itself. There is a small sluiceway on the right. Port-a-Potties are near the sluiceway.

UXBRIDGE

A walk along the top of the dam provides views of a wetlands area. At the end of the dam is a trail that leads into the woods and offers views of seasonal streams and huge boulders. There are rocks and tree roots in the trail.

The woods trail that begins at the dam brings you to the swimming area, and loops around through woodland and open fields back to the dam. There is no fee if you enter the swimming area by this route in the summer, a half mile walk.

At the entrance to the swimming area, accessed from Quaker St. in Uxbridge, there is a kiosk with maps that indicate additional trails. Many of these trails on the far side of the swimming area are wet and overgrown.

Hunting season is from October 16 to April 1. Wear orange while hiking during this time. No hunting allowed on Sundays.

At West Hill Park swimming area children under 10 must be accompanied by parents, guardians, or other adults. No lifeguards. The park season opens the third Saturday of May and closes the second Sunday of September. No dogs are allowed at the swimming area, per the Board of Health. The entrance fee to the Park is $1 per person over 13, maximum $4 per carload.

Call the ranger's office at 508-278-2511 for more information. West Hill Dam has family nature programs ongoing throughout the year.

UXBRIDGE

SNETT Uxbridge

Notable: Rock cuts, pond. Very walkable, undeveloped railtrail.

Trail Map: Available from Mass.gov website—Division of Conservation and Recreation (DCR).

GPS Coordinates: 42°2'34.53"N, 71°38'7.87"W

UXBRIDGE

<u>Directions</u>: Rt. 16 west to Rt. 146 south (just west of Uxbridge Center); travel 2 miles to the Chocolog exit, turn right onto Chocolog Road, fork at .25 miles, bear left to stay on Chocolog another .1 mile, look for SNETT road signs, crossing gates for SNETT, parking on side of road. SNETT on both sides of road.

<u>Cost</u>: None.

<u>Best time to visit</u>: Year round.

<u>Trail Conditions</u>: Unimproved, graded dirt track railbed, wide, open, relatively flat, some sandy spots.

<u>Distance</u>: 3 miles west to Douglas State Forest, 1.5 miles east, blocked by Rt. 146. No access east to other sections of the SNETT across highway presently.

This is a continuation of the trail that originates in Franklin, MA and travels to Douglas, passing through Bellingham, Blackstone, Millville, and Uxbridge before its terminus in Douglas State Park. This section of the SNETT has very few grade crossings, with limited parking access, but allows for a more enjoyable ride when traveling by bike.

The trail is broad and level, with some examples of interesting stonework in the retaining walls, which were constructed when the railroad was built.

Parking at the Chocolog road crossing of the SNETT is extremely limited, basically a road pull-off next to the gated entrance on both sides of the road. Use care when pulling off the road next to the trail; do not block trail gates.

Wrentham

WRENTHAM

Joe's Rock and Birchwold Farms

Notable: View of surrounding countryside from top of Joe's Rock. Migrating waterfowl in pond below Joe's Rock in spring. Broad open fields at Birchwold Farms. Woodcock courtship flights in spring.

Trail Map; Not available presently.

GPS Coordinates: 42°1'45.02"N, 71°24'24.95"W

Directions: From Wrentham Center, Rt. 140, take 1A south. At Rt. 121 junction, take right fork to follow Rt. 121 into Sheldonville area of Wrentham. Continue another 2 miles, looking for large sign on

WRENTHAM

right for Joe's Rock. Immediately past this parking lot is parking on left for Birchwold Farms.

From Bellingham direction, take Wrentham Road away from south Bellingham, follow to end, turn left onto Rt. 121. Birchwold Farms is on right about 100 yards, Joe's Rock on left.

Cost: None.

Best time to visit: Year round.

Trail Conditions: Unimproved dirt track. Trail alongside pond at Joe's Rock has many roots and trip hazards. Trail up to Joe's Rock is steep in places, water bars washed out to some extent. Trails at Birchwold Farms are unimproved dirt track.

Distance: To top of Joe's Rock, .5 mile; along edge of pond, .5 mile; below Joe's Rock, .5 mile. Birchwold Farms trails .5 miles.

490 feet in elevation, Joe's Rock provides a view northeast toward Boston and southwest over the Rhode Island countryside. Next to the parking area, the trail crosses a small stream that must be traversed by walking along a foot-wide board. The trail immediately forks right and left. The right fork heads to the top of Joe's Rock, and the left meanders along the shore of the pond.

Numerous tree roots cross the trail. Steep, somewhat washed-out water bars on route to the top of Joe's Rock. An additional trail goes underneath Joe's Rock, reached by heading up as though to climb toward the Rock, then taking the trail that forks left down toward the shore.

Directly across the street from Joe's Rock is Birchwold Farms, 129 acres of conservation property of varied landscape. Trails skirt the huge open field

WRENTHAM

and lead off into the woods. In these woods are interesting rock outcroppings,

There is ample parking at Birchwold Farm, allowing for a horse trailer or two. Trails are usable for horseback riding (and walking). Additional trails may traverse private property.

WRENTHAM

Knuckup Hill

Notable: View of Boston skyline on clear days.

Trail Map: Not available presently.

GPS Coordinates: 42° 3'9.67"N, 71°19'36.39"W

Directions: Address: 400 Taunton St. Wrentham. From Wrentham Center Rt. 140, traverse town common to Taunton St. Go south about .75 mile past schools complex and look for Senior Center on right. Park at Senior Center, or follow DPW road (to right of Senior Center) to base of Knuckup Hill.

Or from Rt. 495 take Exit 15 (1A) north toward Wrentham Center. Go through intersection with Rt.

WRENTHAM

121, continue on 1A, look for Beach St. on right. Follow Beach to the T with Taunton St., turn left. Wrentham Senior Center is on left about .5 mile farther on Taunton St. Follow road from Senior Center to DPW building .1 mile, park on side of road, fire road climbs straight up to Knuckup Hill on right.

Cost: None.

Bathrooms: At Senior Center when open.

Best time to visit: Year round.

Trail Conditions: Unimproved dirt track-fire road, relatively wide.

Distance: .5 mile.

On clear days you can easily spot the office towers of downtown Boston by standing to the far left at the top of Knuckup Hill; look to the far right.

One trailhead begins at the right of the Senior Center driveway about 20 yards back from Taunton St. A "Warner Trail" leads through the woods on a path that is relatively flat until it joins what is clearly a dirt fire road. This road goes to the top of the hill.

After reaching the fire road, head uphill, follow to near the top of the hill. A smaller foot-trail branches off to the right and leads into a clearing, where you will find remnants of old ski lift equipment, and the view.

Parking next to Trout Pond reduces your hike through woodland and offers a route straight up the fire road that goes to the top of Knuckup Hill. Simply follow the fire road to the top of the hill, watch for the abandoned ski-lift mechanism and turn right, where the view opens up. Beware of poison ivy throughout the area.

WRENTHAM

Trout Pond

Notable: Stone walls, an old spillway, varied terrain. Circular trail.

Trail Map: Not available presently.

GPS Coordinates: 42°3'13.16"N, 71°19'45.51"W

Directions: Address: 400 Taunton St. Wrentham. From Wrentham Center Rt. 140, traverse Wrentham town common to Taunton St. Head south about .75 mile, past schools complex, look for Senior Center on right. Park at Senior Center, or follow DPW road past the Senior Center. DPW building is on the right, and Trout Pond is on the left.

Or, Rt. 495 Exit 15 (1A) head north toward Wrentham Center. Go through intersection with Rt. 121, continue on 1A, look for Beach St. on right. Follow Beach to the T at Taunton St., turn left. Wrentham Senior Center is on left about .5 mile farther on Taunton St. Follow road from Senior Center to DPW building .1 mile, Trout Pond is on left.

Cost: None.

Best time to visit: Access open year round.

Trail Conditions: Unimproved dirt track, graded, wide paths.

Distance: .2 mile.

Take the DPW-paved road that branches off to the right of the Senior Center and park on the side of the road within sight of Trout Pond for a quick stroll. It is possible to walk around the entire pond (actually two small ponds with a walkway between them).

Trout Pond and Knuckup Hill are in such close proximity that for some nice variety, combine the two walks into a single outing.

Woonsocket, RI

WOONSOCKET, R.I.

Blackstone River Bikeway

<u>Notable</u>: Waterfalls along railtrail. Look for water fowl and remnants of the Blackstone River Canal. Longest trail listed in this book. Handicapped accessible.

<u>Trail Map</u>: Available on Blackstone River Valley Heritage Corridor website.

<u>GPS Coordinates</u>: 42°0'8.27"N, 71°29'55.34"W

WOONSOCKET, R.I.

Directions: From Rt. 146 north take Rt. 99 to Rt. 122, (end of Rt. 99—Woonsocket) and turn left onto Rt. 122 Cumberland St. Go through several lights to light at Hamlet St. bridge. Turn left at the light, cross bridge, and take immediate left at next light. Look for "River's Edge Recreational Complex" sign on left.

From Bellingham, take Rt. 126 south (S. Main St.) to Pulaski Boulevard (still Rt. 126), bearing right at Crooks Corner intersection. Continue on Rt. 126 past Stop & Shop Plaza, bearing right to stay on Rt. 126 into Rhode Island. At Social and Clinton streets (the Social Street Flatlands), bear right onto Social St. one block; take first left onto Cumberland St., go past the Cass Avenue light. At next light, turn right onto Hamlet St., cross Hamlet St. bridge. Take immediate first left past the bridge, parking lot is immediately on left. Look for large blue sign saying "River's Edge Recreation Complex."

Cost: None.

Bathrooms: At snack bar near trailhead in Woonsocket when open and at Kelley Museum, Cumberland-Lincoln line, when open.

Best time to visit: Year-round, unplowed in winter. Opportunity for cross-country skiing.

Trail Conditions: Paved railtrail, few road crossings.

Distance: 14 miles from Woonsocket to Central Falls.

The 14 miles of bike trail along the Blackstone River Bikeway has few grade crossings. The Bikeway, part of the Blackstone River Valley National Heritage Corridor, ties in to River's Edge Recreation Complex in Woonsocket, with parking adjacent to the Hamlet St. bridge in Woonsocket, as well as several other parking spots along the trail as you head south into Cumberland and Lincoln, RI.

In winter, the gates to the Woonsocket recreation complex are closed, but walkers and skiers are welcome. Beware of packed down icy areas.

The Blackstone River flows directly next to the Woonsocket-owned recreation area, which offers a small playground, modest putting greens, a building with a snack bar and rest rooms in season, and an additional parking area adjacent to the putting greens.

Along many parts of this northern section of the trail the river is in sight. Cormorants, geese and mallards populate the river, while migrating waterfowl visit in spring and fall. Look for muskrats, ospreys, great blue herons, mergansers and bluebirds. The bikeway is paved, often shady, with benches, pull-off spots, and views of the river and waterfalls along the length of the trail. Blackberries and raspberries along trail in late summer.

Resources

Websites come and go. Look for additional information by searching for the websites of the organizations that oversee properties in this area. Suggested organizations include:

Massachusetts Audubon Society

Trustees of the Reservation

Blackstone Valley Heritage Corridor

Friends of the SNETT

Friends of the Upper Charles

Friends of Choate Park

U.S. Army Corps of Engineers

Friends of Hopedale Parkland

You may also find information about area trails by searching these topics: state recreation sites, Department of Conservation and Recreation (DCR) in MA or specific town websites. Look for town forests in specific towns.

Some towns have extensive information about their conservation properties, especially Wrentham and Franklin, MA. Check town websites and look under "Conservation Department."

Disclaimer: The author and contributors to this book make no representation of accuracy of content, nor guarantee rights of access to any places described herein. Users of this book indemnify and hold harmless the author and contributors.

Notes

Made in the USA
Charleston, SC
15 September 2014